Queen for a Night
Text © 2020 by Stephen Steele Jackson
Illustrations © 2021 by Lily Quintana

All rights reserved. No part of this publication may be reproduced in any manner, stored in a retrieval system, stored in a database and / or published in any form or by any means, electronic, mechanical, photocopying, recording or otherwise, without the prior written permission of the publisher.

ISBN Hardback: 978-0-578-91534-0
ISBN Digital: 978-0-578-91535-7

"For those of you out there who need just a little bit of confidence. I hope you find your true self and continue to show the world how amazing you are, no matter who you decide to be!" **-Stephen Steele Jackson**

Special THANKS to Connie, Emily, Gillian, and Mom for your support!

"For all those people who have unfulfilled dreams. The only way to make them come true is to be brave and fight for them with faith, love and self-confidence, eliminating the obstacles that we impose on ourselves with our fears. Only in this way will our path be clear, and we will reach our goals before we know it because life rewards brave people." **-Lily Quintana**

Max is just like any other 10-year-old boy. He loves to climb trees, play outside with his friends, and go fishing with his Dad.

...is watching his Mom put on her makeup.

To Max, watching his Mom put on makeup is like watching an artist create a live painting.

The next day at school, Max's teacher told the class about the school's upcoming talent show. All the kids were signing up and talking about their acts. Mary was going to dance, Sarah was going to sing, and David was going to tell a few jokes!

"Are you going to sign up, Max?" his teacher asked.

Max shrugged. "Not sure I can perform on stage by MYSELF!"

"You'll be fine!" she exclaimed. "Now, let's sign you up, shall we?"

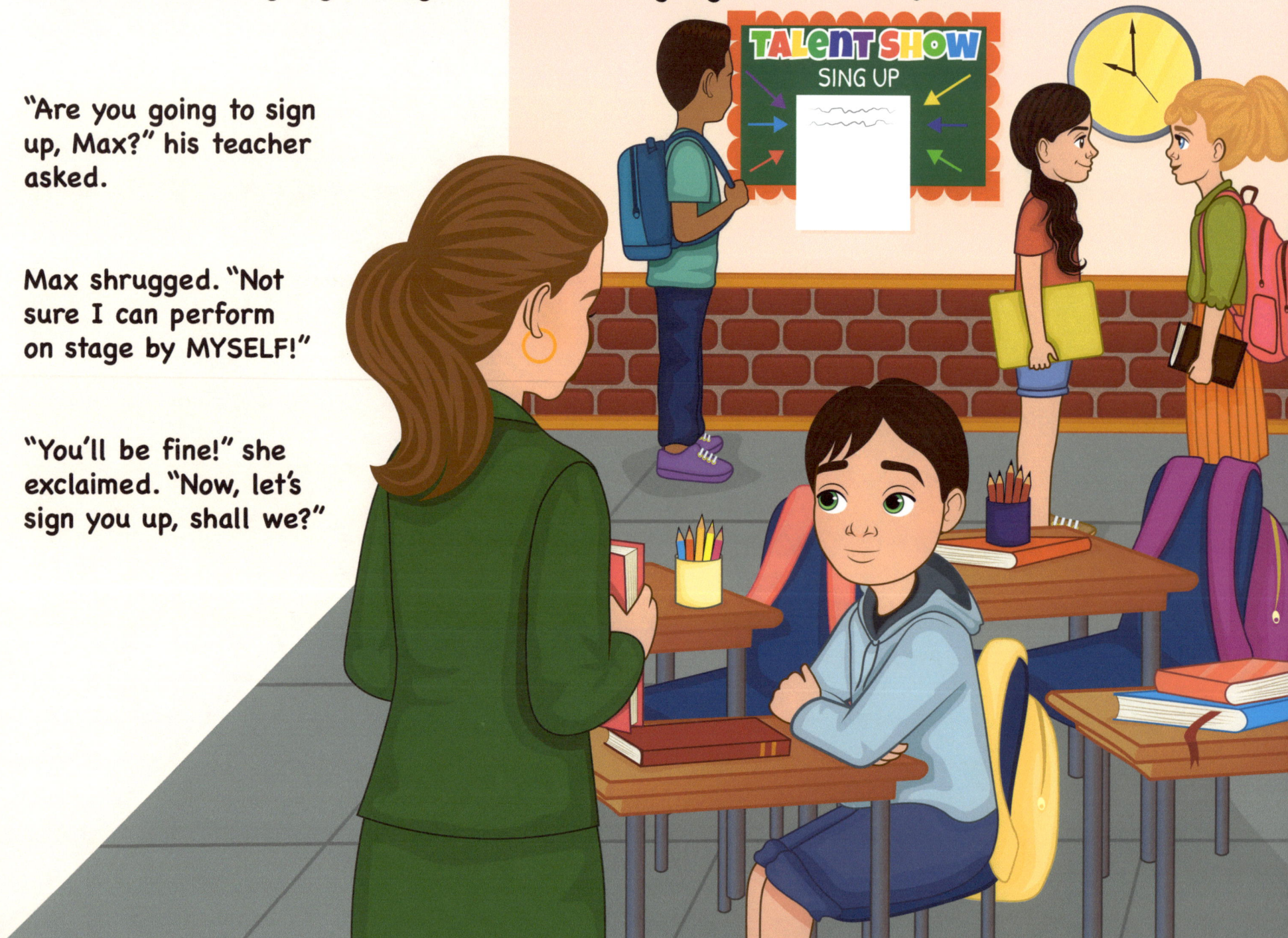

The rest of the day, Max was overcome with fear. The thought of singing by himself seemed like the scariest thing in the world.

Then it hit him! He remembered what his Mom told him about makeup.

"What if I wear make up?" he thought to himself. "Maybe it will make me feel more confident?"

That afternoon when Max got home, his parents were still at work. Realizing he was all alone, he knew this was the perfect opportunity to practice putting on makeup. So Max snuck into his Mom's room and sat down at her vanity. He had seen her put on makeup many times before and figured it shouldn't be too hard.

Max took out the pallet of eye makeup that had every array of pigments imaginable. He dabbed a brush into the colors called pink blossom and purple rain and smeared them all over his eyelids. Then, to finish off his look, he took out his Mom's brightest red lipstick and applied it to his lips.

Staring into the mirror, Max was shocked. "Not bad for my first try," he chuckled.

Finally, Max put on one of his Mom's fancy dresses, grabbed a hairbrush, and began to sing and dance all over her room. Just then...

"MAX!" his mother shouted. "What do you think you are doing, playing with my makeup? And look at the mess you made... and on your face!"

Feeling embarrassed, Max dropped his head in defeat as tears began to roll down his face.

"Max, honey," she spoke softly. "You know you aren't allowed to wear Mommy's clothes and play with her makeup without permission. They are very expensive."

"I just wanted to feel confident and beautiful like you, Mom," uttered Max.

"Why do you say that?" she asked.

Max sniffled. "Well, there is this talent show at school, and all of the other kids are signing up. I want to be in the show, but I'm scared I don't have what it takes." he confessed. "That's why I thought putting on your makeup would help. If it can help you feel confident, then maybe it could help me?"

"Oh, Max!" she said soothingly. "Why didn't you just talk to me?"

Max shrugged his shoulders. "I guess I was just a little embarrassed to talk to you about it."

Max's mom grinned. "I have an idea!"

The next day after school, Max's Mom picked him up for a special trip.

"Where are we going?" questioned Max.

"I have a good friend whom I think can help you." hinted Mom as she winked mischievously at Max.

A few minutes later, they arrived. Max looked up in awe as he saw the rainbow-colored storefront and a large sign that read...

Miss Lexi's
Costume and Design Emporium Extravaganza

While walking into the shop, Max was speechless. He had never seen so many sparkling outfits all in one place.

Just then, a short, blond-haired woman, wearing a beautiful pink dress and matching high heels came from the back room.

"Just in time, Sharon!" Miss Lexi rejoiced. "I was wondering if you two were still coming."

"Miss Lexi, this is my son, Max, whom I told you about," Mom replied.

"Aw, yes!" Miss Lexi said. "I've heard many great things about you, Max. I've also been told that you have a talent show coming up. Is that correct?" she questioned.

"Yes, ma'am," stated Max.

"Well, honey, you have come to the right place!" she declared. "Do you know what kind of shop this is, Max?"

"Not really," he said with uncertainty.

"Max," his Mom interrupted. "I was telling Miss Lexi last night how much you loved to play dress-up and watch me put on makeup and how you seemed interested in maybe doing your makeup for the talent show."

"Is that so, Max?" Miss Lexi asked as she looked down at Max, whose face was beginning to come to life.

Max began to bubble! "I've always been interested in makeup. I watch my Mom do hers all the time. I just thought boys couldn't wear makeup." he speculated.

"Here's what I think," says Miss Lexi. "Makeup has no gender. Many people, both guys and girls, wear makeup all the time. Like when you watch a movie or TV show. Everyone is wearing makeup. You just might not be able to tell. For me," she adds, "wearing makeup is my way of showing the world who I am, even before I have to say anything at all. And as a DRAG QUEEN, it's my art, and it's my way of expressing my true self." Miss Lexi pauses...

"When I put on my makeup before a show, I can transform myself from a timid and shy, short little man named ALEX to Miss Lexi! A fierce and confident queen who isn't afraid of anything."

"That's why I brought you here, Max." his Mom said. "If you are truly interested in wearing makeup and a fancy dress for your talent show, Miss Lexi has graciously offered her assistance. But I want you to know," she expressed as she took Max's hand, "No matter what you decide, Dad and I will love and support you every step of the way."

Grinning from ear to ear, Max shouted, "Can I wear a wig, too?"

"Absolutely!" his mom said.

Max shouted out with glee as he dashed around the store, checking out all the dazzling things "Miss Lexi's Costume and Design Emporium Extravaganza" has to offer.

The next few days after school, Max's Mom invited Alex (Miss Lexi) to their house to help Max practice for the upcoming talent show.

First, Alex asked Max to show him the song he was going to perform. He picked his favorite, "The Way I Was Born" by Lady Gee.

Next, Alex showed Max how to walk in heels. Watching from inside the kitchen, Max's Mom and Dad giggled as Max stumbled around the house. Alex thought it would be fun if Max's dad practiced walking as well. So, he took out his heels and handed them to Dad.

"Look at you go!" Max's Mom shouted out to Dad. "You walk better in heels than I do."

"That's surprising for someone who played college football," snickered Alex as he grinned at Max.

"Well, you know," Dad replied, "they made the entire football team in college take ballet. Said it would help our balance."

"Then maybe I should take ballet class, too!" Max said with glee.

After strutting around the house for several minutes, Alex helped Max choreograph dance moves to go with his song. Max was a natural!

Overcome with joy, Alex sang out, "I think he's ready!"

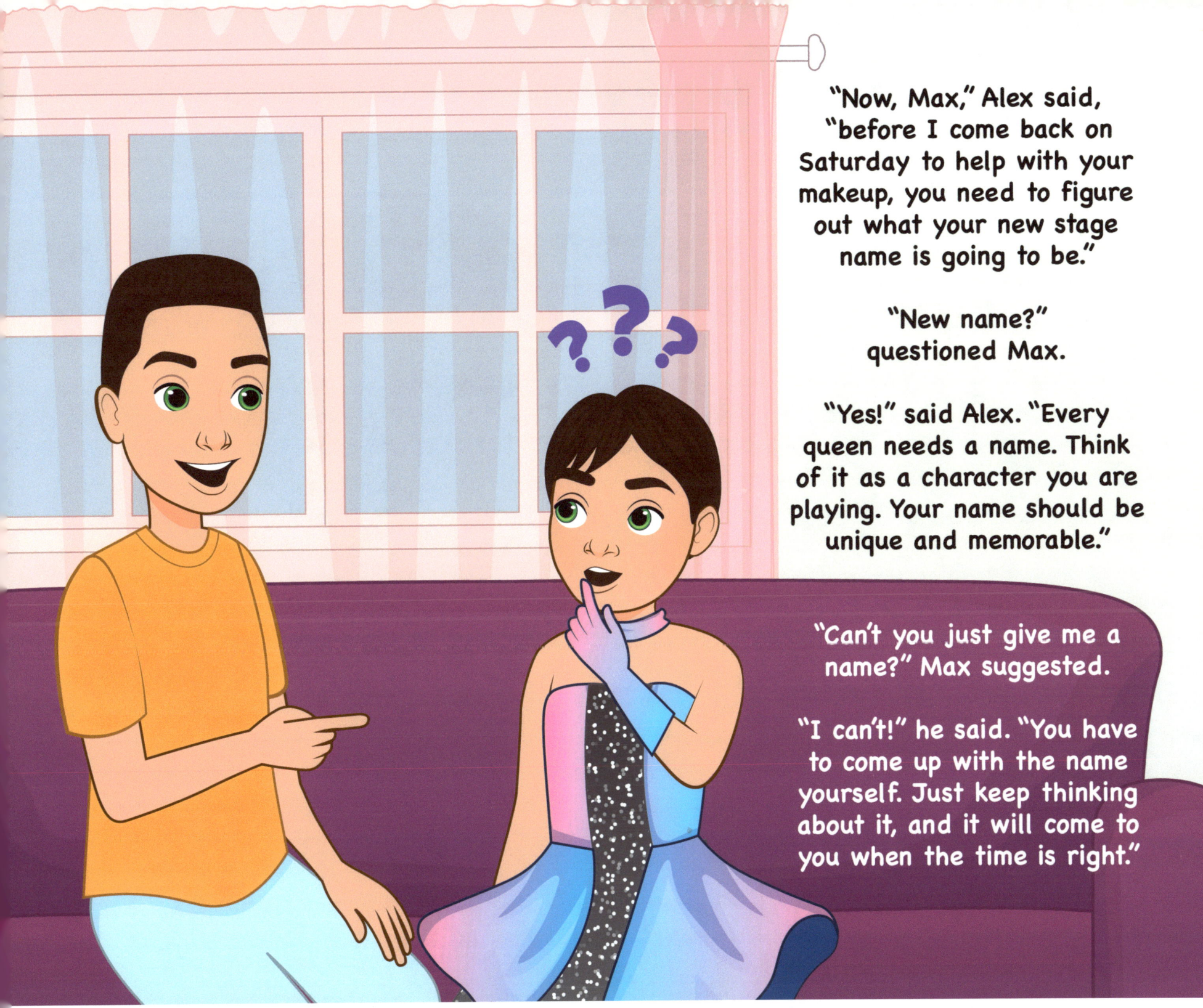

"Now, Max," Alex said, "before I come back on Saturday to help with your makeup, you need to figure out what your new stage name is going to be."

"New name?" questioned Max.

"Yes!" said Alex. "Every queen needs a name. Think of it as a character you are playing. Your name should be unique and memorable."

"Can't you just give me a name?" Max suggested.

"I can't!" he said. "You have to come up with the name yourself. Just keep thinking about it, and it will come to you when the time is right."

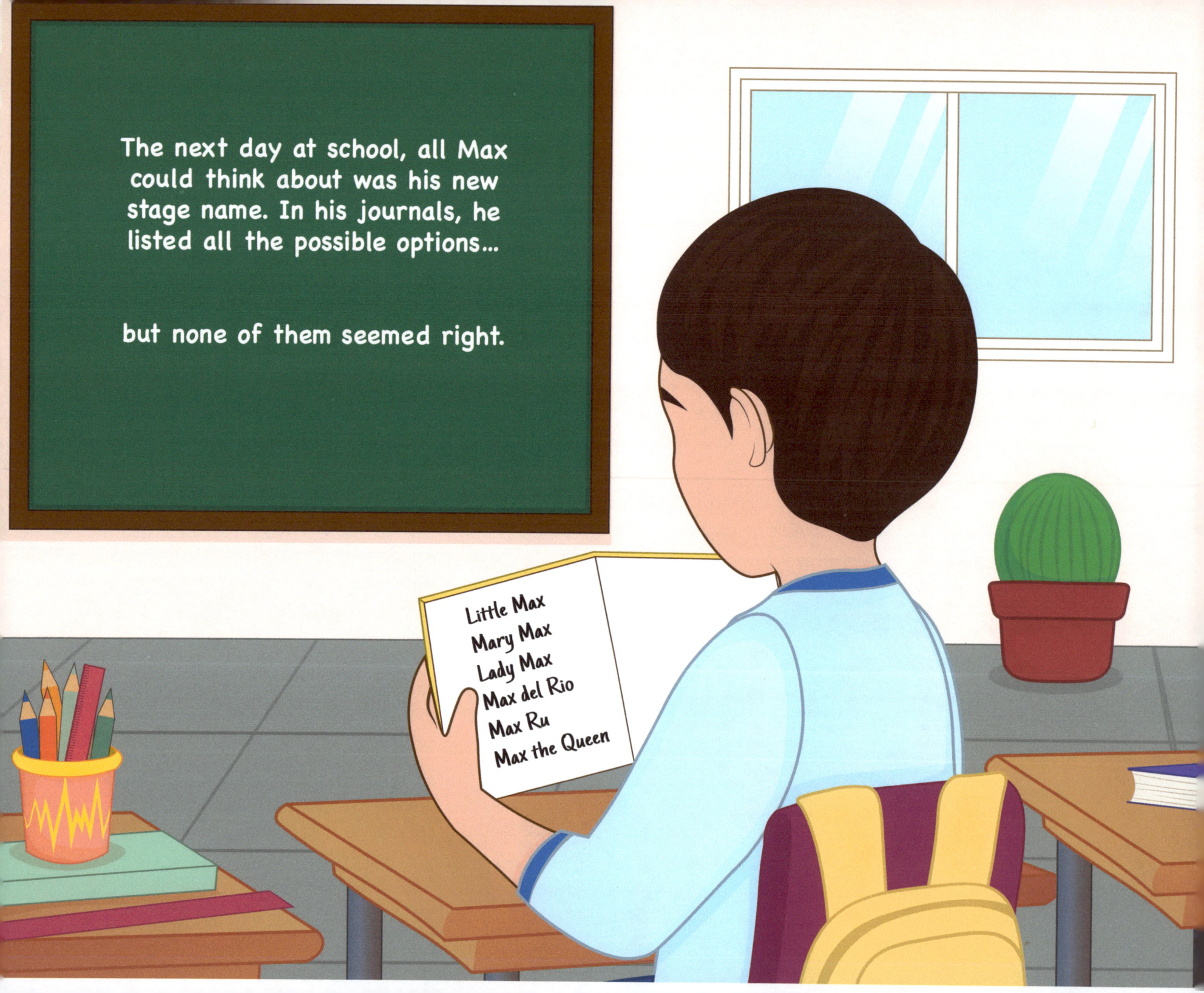

Finally, as he was getting ready to go home, Max overheard Sarah boasting about her act and how she couldn't wait to be "seen" by everyone. She told David that she was singing her favorite song, "The Way I was Born" by Lady Gee.

Max's heart sank. He had worked so hard on his act, and now Sarah was performing the same song.

"I'll never be good enough, now!" Max said, dragging his feet out of the classroom.

That afternoon when Mom got home, she knew something was wrong with Max! Tomorrow was the big day, and he had been very excited, up until now.

"Max, why are you so sad?" Mom asked.

"Well," he sighed. "Sarah is singing the same song that I am, and she is perfect. There is no way I'm going to do well, now!"

"So, what if Sarah is doing the same song as you? Your act is better than hers!" she reassured. "All that matters is that you have fun on that stage."

The following day, Miss Lexi arrived with all of her drag essentials in tow.

"Moving in, I see." jested Dad.

Miss Lexi chuckled. "If you think this is moving in, then honey, you need a bigger house! Why do you think I had to open up my very own costume and wig shop?" she added.

"I don't know if we can handle having two DIVAS in the house," Mom said while giving Dad a friendly pat on the back.

"Ha, ha, ha, very funny!" snickered Dad.

"Where's Max?" Miss Lexi asked as she looked around.

Just then,
Max plodded down
the stairs and into the kitchen.

"Oh, Max, honey! What's the matter?" Miss Lexi said.

For the next several minutes, Max told Miss Lexi what had happened the day before and how Sarah was doing the same song. Then he explained how he was now more unsure of himself than ever.

Knowing exactly what to say, she told Max, "Do you know how many times someone has performed the same song as me? It's nerve-racking, but it's a chance for you to STAND OUT!" she added. You will do it better than Sarah. You just have to believe in yourself."

"I don't know," Max said anxiously. "I just want to be seen for who I really am."

"How about we get started on that makeup?" Miss Lexi said. "I think it will help you see things differently."

Max's face lit up again. Finally, his favorite part!

Sitting at the same vanity in his Mom's room where it all started, Miss Lexi painted Max's face and used all of his favorite colors. Finally, Miss Lexi had Max try on his costume and wig.

When Max looked in the mirror, he couldn't believe the transformation. "I look so different!" He exclaimed. "I love it!"

"You look FIERCE!" Miss Lexi added.

Starting to doubt himself again, he asked, "Do you think the other kids are going to laugh and make fun of me?"

Overcome with emotions, Miss Lexi sat Max down and looked him in the eyes. "People are always going to laugh and make fun of others. That's just the world we live in. Sometimes they do it because they are insecure of their own feelings. Sometimes they do it to try and fit in. But no matter what, if they are laughing at you, it's because they are jealous!" she explained. "Jealous of people like us who are not afraid to be our true selves!"

"What if I lose my friends?" Max asked nervously.

"If they don't want be your friend because you decided to be a fierce and confident queen on stage for a night, then they weren't your friends to begin with," she sassed. "Friends will come and go throughout your entire life, but there is only one YOU! So be the person you want to be friends with."

Max looked up at Miss Lexi and smiled with confidence. "Let's go show my parents my new look!"

Max strutted into the kitchen to show off his newfound confidence! Both of his parents cheered and clapped with approval. Max beamed with joy, knowing his parents truly accepted him.

"Max!" Miss Lexi said. "I almost forgot. Did you ever come up with a name?"

"I did. Just now!" He confirmed.

"Well, what is it?" Mom asked.

Mary tap danced off beat... David's jokes weren't landing...

and Sarah sang well.

Now it was Max's turn! He was super nervous, still unsure if he could go through singing and dancing as "MaxScene." But when the lights came up, and it was time for him to step onto the stage, Max was nowhere to be seen...

MaxScene sang and danced his heart out that night and had the entire audience on their feet, clapping and dancing. He was the talk of the show.

After the talent show, Max ran up to Miss Lexi and his parents, and gave them the biggest hug!

"Look, Mom and Dad!" Max shouted. "I did it! Can you believe it?"

"We believed in you this entire time," they both said lovingly.

"Oh, and no one laughed at me either!" he said cheerfully.

"Oh, and one more thing," she added.

Author's Note

Stephen Steele Jackson is an elementary educator and a DRAG QUEEN named Miss Lexi Andrews.

Introducing his first children's book, Queen for a Night is a story that appeals to a large audience of readers, both young and old, especially those struggling to find the confidence to be their true self.

"This story hits very close to home for me, as I was just like Max growing up. Compared to other boys my age, I shared the same love for makeup and expressing myself in a very different way. Unlike Max, when I was a kid, I did not have the same type of support to help guide me when I was exploring my artistically creative side. However, the loving support that came later in life inspired me to become who I am today; an amazing elementary teacher and a FIERCE drag queen."

"It is my hope that this story will help break the traditional stereotypes set upon our world on what a boy or girl can or can't be and encourage open communications between children and their families. In return, I hope it will also help lead children, like Max, on an exploration of finding one's true self without the fear of what others may think."

-Stephen Steele Jackson
(A.K.A. Miss Lexi Andrews)